# The Accidental Mary Pilgrimage

Sue Fitzmaurice

*To Jo.*

# Also by Sue Fitzmaurice

### Fiction

*Angels in the Architecture*

### Non-fiction

*Purpose – the Elements of Purpose.*
*Purpose – Making sure your Purpose finds you.*

## Note to the Reader

In the main I employ *English* English. Those unused to this great language may stumble over the 'u' of neighbour and the verb of 'practise'. There is no word 'gotten' in the Queen's English and we politely 'minimise' without a 'z' (which we pronounce 'zed', by the way). Quotations from others are in the version of English of their nationality or first publication. Any other errors are indeed mine and I pray your forgiveness.

*Candles to the Madonna, Montserrat*

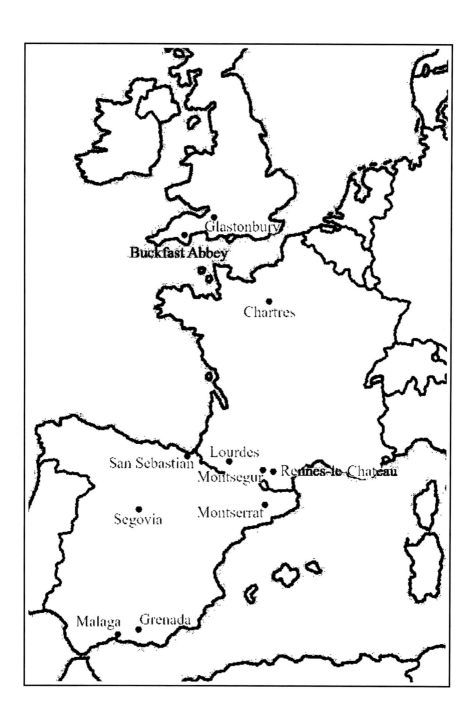

# Contents

## Introduction

**Acknowledgements**

**About the Authors**

# Introduction

I've visited many holy places and spiritual centres in my life and enjoyed them all. Two of the most moving ever have been the Baha'i Faith's *Shrine of the Bab* in Haifa in northern Israel, and the *Dongyu Gatsal* Tibetan Buddhist nunnery in Himachal Pradesh in northern India *(below)*. In both cases they were astoundingly sweet experiences. When I first entered the Shrine of the Bab twenty years ago, I remember feeling as though I was at the centre of the universe,

 such was the clearness of the energy I felt there. At *Dongyu Gatsal*, I visited the temple just as the young nuns went in for their daily chanting and prayer, and I sat on the floor for an hour and listened and was transported away to I know not where – it was stunningly beautiful. It sits in the foothills of the Himalayas with one of the most astounding views of those great peaks from the steps of the temple. The energy is powerfully feminine and pristine.

When I talk about the 'energy' of a place, it has to do with the feelings I experience when I'm there. Although saying that it's just feelings isn't quite the whole story either. It's not something that you experience from the inside – it's something that comes *at* you from

the outside. And it touches your heart and soul. And you then experience that as some feelings, sometimes very clear and specific, sometimes more general.

I visit any such places with great appreciation, admiration and respect, and if I'm lucky I get to lap up something deliciously energising.

I don't have that experience in every religious place – sometimes the feeling is heavy and dark, sometimes there's no feeling in particular. But my curiosity for it will always remain. I've been fascinated with religion since I was a small child, seeking out the knowledge and experience of *all* of the world's great Faiths, and many of their denominations and sects. As a result, my belief has for a long time been very universalist – there is Truth in all the great Faiths, although I don't believe any are exclusive of the others and indeed I believe they are all connected to the one God, the one Universe, the Divine. Where one has acted to oppress then I see only that some of its practitioners – or more particular some of its hierarchy – have moved too far away from their own essence. Where there is joy and Light, then they've simply maintained their proximity to the Divine.

At the beginning of 2018 I found myself in the midst of an English winter, in Plymouth in Devon, wondering what on Earth I was doing there. I'd been traveling off and on for two years – I always say my children grew up and *I* left home – and my intention had been to be in the southern hemisphere at that time of year, enjoying a New Zealand and Australian summer. So it was a bit of a mystery to me how I'd ended up being in the exact opposite climate and on the opposite side of the world. I thought there must be some reason this had happened, since nothing seemed to happen in my life anymore without purpose, so I was waiting to see what that was all about. In the meantime I wrote, and snuggled up with two cuddly dogs I was babysitting, and went for long walks around Plymouth.

Plymouth isn't the most exciting place in England and I was trying to convince a friend in London to come visit for a week to break a little of the tedium. I'd also messaged Jo, a Facebook friend of a few years, who I knew was somewhere in the south of England and lived – as a musician – a somewhat transient life, not dissimilar to my own.

As it turned out, Jo had a BBC radio interview coming up in Plymouth, with a gig the next night at a pub in Totnes, a half hour away, so she accepted my invitation straightaway and planned to come down for a week. The day Jo was due to arrive – she had a long drive across from the south-east – it had been raining buckets and I messaged her and said 'drive safe!' A couple of hours later she messaged me back to say she'd had an accident, although she was alright and her car was alright but she was a bit shaken and would be taking it slowly and would take a bit longer to get there. Later on, returning from my usual morning dog walk, I was wandering around

*Sainsburys* looking for something and I had the strangest feeling that I was going to have to go and rescue Jo. Not five minutes later she phoned to say she was a bit shaken up and could I catch a train to Exeter and drive her and her car back to Plymouth. Bear in mind we'd never met and had only ever exchanged a few words on Messenger, so I knew she wouldn't be asking lightly. I dashed home, quickly cleaned two very dirty dogs, and eventually got on a train to Exeter. By the time I arrived, she'd recovered and we toddled on back to Plymouth.

We had a lovely week, which included two days exploring magical Dartmoor *(below)* with the doggos, and we generally relaxed and hung out. It was very unpressured and we had a good few laughs. What could be better.

A week later, Jo left early back to the south-east, and I headed across to Portsmouth to take the ferry the next day across the Channel to France for my next house sit in the south. We figured we'd probably meet up again sometime, but who knew when that would be.

As it turned out, a lot sooner than we'd thought. Jo had been working on releasing her first full-length album and about a week later she asked me to look at a documentary video she'd made and we ended up chatting about it live over Messenger. It was apparent that Jo was pretty stressed by her workload, and it was without much difficulty that I talked her into coming to France. She would be able to do everything she needed to from a distance and she'd be in a lovely peaceful place to chill out. So only two weeks after we'd parted in Plymouth, Jo flew into Toulouse, supposedly for a week. That was the thirteenth of February. We took the ferry back across the channel together on the twenty-fifth of March. In the intervening six weeks, we drove down from the north of Spain to the south-east, back up the east coast, through the Pyrenees and up through the centre of France. I also went to Morocco for a week. It was probably the most adventurous six weeks of my life, and in a way, it's still carrying on.

As I wrote the substantive part of this book, we were both in Manchester; Jo was writing and recording her *next* album downstairs in the study of the lovely mansion house flat where we were minding two extremely laidback lurchers. It was Spring by then and we'd missed the bulk of the severe English winter. We were experiencing a burst of unexpected creativity. In fact, *unexpected* pretty much sums it all up.

It's amazing when you look back and realise how nothing is an accident.

# 1. Buckfast Abbey, England

It was only in retrospect that we realised our accidental pilgrimage really started with our visit to Buckfast Abbey on the eastern edge of Dartmoor in England. I'd skirted part of Dartmoor eighteen months earlier and I'd very much wanted to have more of an explore, especially as it was 'right there', just north of Plymouth. Jo knew her way around parts of it, so after her work engagements were successfully completed and we'd had a quiet day off, we headed out early one morning to the moor, dogs happily in tow.

As is typical with the moor, we left Plymouth in sunshine and it quickly turned into low cloud, heavy mizzle and fog. Our first stop was for coffee in Princetown, pretty deserted except for The Old Police Station café. We took the dogs in with us, although we weren't entirely sure how these two excitable wee furballs were

going to behave. They were very good, although Woody did escape being tied up under the table without us noticing; the escapee was returned to us by one of the kitchen staff, where he'd made a beeline apparently. You've never seen such an innocent face.

From there we carried on through the moor, stopping at various places to climb tors (hills topped with outcrops of rock), which the dogs *loved*. Chloe could run off the lead – Woody was not to be trusted – but they both had an absolute ball and were thoroughly muddy and exhausted by the time we got them home. Some people find the moor depressing – I think it's amazing. Its gloominess is part of what makes it so profound, and the land seems very powerful.

Our last stop was to Buckfast Abbey. As we arrived, the clouds broke and the beautiful late afternoon winter sun showed us Buckfast in the best of all possible lights. Better than a postcard really.

The first Benedictine abbey began here in 1018 – a thousand years ago! It was lost in the dissolution in 1539 and destroyed. The site was purchased by a group of French Benedictine monks in 1882 and the current abbey and monastic buildings were begun in 1907.

The church was consecrated in 1932 and completed in 1938. This is possibly what accounts for its incredible lightness. The interior is white and its energy is crystal clear and simple and sweet and crisp. It was the loveliest feeling to sit there and I felt I could have stayed a very long time.

Not until we looked back at that trip three months later did we realise we had indeed sat with *Our Lady of Buckfast* that day.

And then there was this guy:

Who was pretty magnificent, with his 8-metre wide welcome.

The abbey is entirely self-sufficient, with gardens, a working farm, a restaurant and shops. The monks produce Buckfast tonic wine which has inadvertently done well as an alcohol of choice among some Scottish teenagers. We bought a bottle – it's very tasty.

That was the end of that day on Dartmoor but given a range of several choices for another day trip out two days later, we actually went up to Dartmoor again and explored more of it. Not the least of our second day's adventures was *Grimspound,* ruins of a bronze age village dating from 1300BC. Driving there, the fog grew thicker, and by the time we arrived we could only see about 20 feet in front of us. We were a bit apprehensive about walking the few hundred metres away from our car towards where we thought the village was (which was basically where Google Maps said it was, and Google wasn't *always* right), given there wasn't actually a path or any signs. It was pretty much in a straight line though, and well worth it.

There are 24 stone huts in a circle surrounded by a stone wall about 150 metres in diameter. It's very eerie, although not in an especially heavy or scary way – it's just mysterious. Given the conditions though you'd have been excused for finding it creepy.

I couldn't help thinking about the lives of the people that had lived there, and the conditions of living year-round at the top of the moor. This wasn't a hospitable place, despite that it had its own power. It had to have been very strategically placed, isolated and hard to find. It seemed as though there were perhaps a few former inhabitants around still.

I'm fascinated by the building of things. Be it bridges or new highways or 3,000-year-old villages or cathedrals. The engineering of it intrigues me. I can be as cynical as the next person about the human cost of things like cathedrals – my novel *Angels in the Architecture* looks especially at the human sacrifice – but I choose to put that aside as much as I can in order to explore what else is there.

One of the many attractions to various parts of Britain for me is the profound history of the place. I come from a very new country, with an indigenous history 'only' several hundred years old, and a European/settler history of much less. The oldest buildings – of which there are only a handful – are less than two hundred years old. That newness gives New Zealand an untouched quality that is extremely attractive. But my DNA is Scottish and Irish and it pulls on me. The Celtic, Gaelic, Arthurian and Druid histories and legends speak to my heart and soul; Dartmoor was yet another magical place to feed those ancient roots. When we left Grimspound and Dartmoor that day, not for the first time I felt very privileged to be exploring the world, about as far away from my birth home as I could go.

*Jo and Woody on Dartmoor – they were rather in love.*

# 2. Lourdes, France.

My house sit in the south of France wasn't far from the famous pilgrimage town of Lourdes. Lourdes is a small town in the foothills of the Pyrenees; it became prominent in 1858 after a peasant girl, Bernadette Soubirous, claimed to have seen the Virgin Mary a total of eighteen times, at the Massabielle grotto. Mary instructed Bernadette to dig in the ground at a certain spot and to drink from the small spring of water that appeared there. Very soon after this, cures were reported from drinking the water, and it's claimed tens of thousands of cures have occurred in the 160 years since. Lourdes hosts five million visitors and pilgrims a year and now has more hotels than any other town or city in France outside Paris.

*Angel clouds above Lourdes.*

So for me, being near to Lourdes – it was about an hour's drive away from where I was staying – was irresistible. Jo hadn't been there before either and I waited till she arrived so we could go together. Given the popularity of Lourdes as a pilgrimage destination, one might fear, as I did, that it had turned into a sort of Euro-Disney of Katholic Kitsch as a result. A few months previously I'd visited Stonehenge in Wiltshire in England and I'd never been so disappointed with something purportedly so magnificent. Aside from what everyone notices, that it's a lot smaller than you think it's going to be, it was a bit too much of an 'exit through the gift shop' experience. Lesser known, and only half an hour's drive away, is Avebury Stone Circle, where visitors can walk in and around the stones in a much less tourist-driven and more atmospheric environment. We wondered if Lourdes was going to be more Stonehenge or more Avebury. We needn't have worried.

It was a gorgeous drive there. The Pyrenees start off as a long alpine line in the distance. There are some unusually shaped peaks – one we nicknamed Mordor for its distinctive shape. Like many such regions, the air is clear and the energy feels untouched.

*The Pyrenees*

It was a great time of year to visit Lourdes as the high season and shoulder season crowds were completely absent. It was a gorgeous sunny winter day and we found a car park within a short walk of the basilica. Only about half the Katholic Kitsch stores were open, and actually we really enjoyed them. We didn't exactly make fun of the plastic Jesuses – truth is, we bought one – but the gift shops were fun, and one imagines it could have been a lot more tasteless and neon than it was. The town is charming enough – hotels weren't towering or overly modern – most things were in keeping with the character of a small French town. The site of the main basilica is beautiful, with parklike grounds along one side, the river to the other, and a campus of sorts with libraries and pilgrim centres.

*Panorama of Lourdes & Basilica*

The main church is the Basilica of our Lady of the Rosary, completed in 1989. It is one of three churches on the site. It's beautiful, stunningly so, but it was as cold as a tomb when we went in, so I didn't stay long. I wandered up the outside stairs at the front of the basilica to see what else there was to see up there. I'd done virtually no research or reading before we went, aside from my usual check around Google Maps. (Where would we be without Google Maps?!) There was a wee sign for *crypte et basilique de l'immaculée conception.* I had enough French to understand that this was the chapel requested by the Virgin Mary when she appeared to Bernadette. As you go in, there is a small chapel to the right commemorating Bernadette herself. Bernadette's visions occurred when she was only 14; she later joined the *Sisters of Charity* and died at age 35 from tuberculosis. She was canonised in 1933.

Returning to the main corridor, there's a tunnel-like walk to the small *Basilica of the Immaculate Conception.* An icon of the Madonna rests above the alter, which itself is directly above the *Grotte de Massabielle*, the shallow cave in the rocky outcrop upon which the basilicas are now built, adjacent to the river. There were just a few other people here and I sat down in a pew near the back. I was immediately aware of the most beautiful and profound energy – it was very obviously maternal, but very no-nonsense, and hugely embracing. I'd never felt anything like it before and I just felt I wanted to stay in it forever. I looked around wondering if others felt the same thing – I got the impression that some of the other devotees there were regulars and they probably did get it and that's why they were there. I thought this must be what the 'cult of Mary', in the Catholic Church in particular, was all about, although it had never seemed to me that this was the nature of the image of Mary cast by Catholicism. Had I misinterpreted that depiction, or was it really that Mary was portrayed as something less than this powerful but that there were those who knew better? I really bathed in the glow of the energy, and I was aware that Jo had come in and sat down across from me. We'd gone wandering our own ways around the place. After a while I got up to leave and so did Jo and we looked at each other with wide eyes, mouthing *Wow!* 'Did you get that?!' 'Yeah, did you?!' 'Yeah!'

From here we meandered down and around to the grotto itself, which was when we realised that the alter of the previous chapel was directly above the grotto. The grotto is set up with rows of seats in front of it, and since it's outside it looks a little odd. It's really just a widening of the rock upon which the basilica was ultimately built. You can walk in and around it – the underground stream that bubbled up there a hundred and sixty years ago is still there and is quite a gushing torrent, covered around now with a Perspex screen; the water itself has been piped into a row of taps along the wall away to the left of the grotto. People were there with multiple large plastic water containers. It does taste very lovely and we filled a small plastic container we'd bought at one of the kitsch shops. We'd got several small bottles too that we filled as gifts for some special friends – they're very sweet, with little metal stamps across the front with the scene of Bernadette kneeling at the grotto before Mary. The same image graced every kind of kitsch you can imagine. We decided to have a competition for best katholic kitsch; I won that day with a six-inch high plastic Jesus who's since travelled everywhere with us – we always set him out on the telly or some such in all the places we've gone. His outstretched arms are useful for hanging bracelets and rings and he seems only too happy to oblige. He's a bit of a rock star really.

After filling our water bottles and stopping by a couple of stores (I bought the first of several bracelets, this one with a wee medallion of Bernadette and a cedarwood cross), we found a café by the river for lunch. I don't remember now what I ate, but I do remember Jo ate egg and chips and I teased her mercilessly about being in France and eating bloody egg and chips. You can take the girl out of England… At my house sit up the road from Lourdes we had four dogs – they were a gorgeous bunch of oddballs, a Weimaraner, a Newfoundland, a Poodle and Bijan, and they had to go into the barn when we went out, and I was very conscious of getting back and letting them out, so after lunch we didn't really have any time to look round Lourdes anymore, but we were very happy nonetheless. With our water and our kitsch.

We still have some of the water. We've used it solely as an aperitif, adding a dash to our gin and tonic. It tastes better that way. The gin, that is.

I want to go back again to Lourdes, and stay longer, especially in that chapel. The feeling of it has stayed with me, and I'm sure it will for a long time, maybe forever. Mary power really won me over that day and I became quite a fan. In fact, in hindsight, we became real groupies – we didn't know it at the time but we were about to spend six weeks following her – and Mary Magdalene – around Europe, on tour.

# 3. San Sebastián, Spain

We had a very relaxing and creative time in France. I finished a new book proposal and Jo wrote several songs for her new album. We toyed with ideas for retreats and new ventures and came up with names and logos, delighting our friends with descriptions of our holiday experiences with dogs, French wine, cocktail afternoons in the sun, dejeuner in the Pyrenees, pyjama days on laptops, and occasionally finding ourselves driving on the wrong side of the road (In Europe the correct side is the right; in the UK and New Zealand it's the left). When our hosts returned we had a couple of days to get to the next house sit in the south of Spain, and our plan was to nip over the border to San Sebastián in the north, just west of the Pyrenees, and then tootle south via Madrid.

En route Jo told me of some of the legends of the Magdalene, not least of which of course is the notion that Mary married Jesus, that they had a child together, and that Mary escaped the holy land and came to France. Some of it is very *Da Vinci Code,* but other stories have emerged out of other traditions entirely. I've

certainly never believed the idea that Mary was a prostitute; it's surely the greatest deliberate historical insult ever against a woman, and one who was almost certainly nobility and definitely a renowned healer and seer in her own right.

It was a little strange driving into Spain; I'd never been there before and I'm increasingly aware that every country – and areas within countries – have their own energy, and you can feel the changes as you traverse them. It was a beautiful, sunny morning on the French side of the Pyrenees and we remarked, as we often had, on the tree-lined avenues that are such a feature of the French countryside. Jo looked up accommodation possibilities in the old part of the San Sebastián while we were en route, as we frustratingly dipped in and out of phone coverage skirting round the Atlantic end of the Pyrenees. We hardly knew when we actually crossed into Spain, so relaxed are the borders between European Union countries. Road signs started to appear in Spanish while we were still in France, but then the French disappeared altogether and we judged from Google Maps that we'd entered Spain. Word to the wise: if you're using Google Maps to find your hotel – or anywhere for that matter – in Spain, make sure you write the address into the search bar **with all the accents on the letters,** because otherwise it may take you somewhere else entirely. Long story short, after a bit of faffing about, we found our hotel.

The old city of San Sebastián is gorgeous – a wee maze of alleyways full of funky shops and tapas bars. Jo had been to Spain before and had been telling me about sangria, a Spanish cocktail of red wine and fruit, with added brandy and/or orange liqueur. The tapas bars all serve their own freshly made sangria, and so you can get variations between bars. You can also buy it at the

supermarket for as little as a euro per litre, even cheaper than wine, and it's delicious. In fact, it probably goes down way too easily if I'm honest. So we found some tapas, drank some sangria, and wandered about the cute wee streets, and around the

harbour promenade. I love being somewhere new and different, and although I was pretty tired from driving it was just great to look around. Quite by accident we crossed an alley that had a beautiful Church peeking out at one end and so we went for a look.

It was the *Iglesia de Santa Maria del Coro*, the oldest Church in San Sebastián,

dedicated to Mary. I'm not particularly familiar with Catholic
churches, and what's been amazing to me about the European
churches and basilicas we were to come across, is that they
mostly have a large central nave, with multiple small chapels
dotted around sometimes all four sides, dedicated to various
saints and archangels, both well-known and more obscure.
There was *always* a chapel dedicated to Saint Mary the Mother,
very often to Saint Mary Magdalene (or Mary Madeleine as she
was often referred to in France and Spain), and other women
saints: Therese, Rita, Anna (the grandmother of Jesus), Barbara,
and so on. I was amazed by this incredible presence of women
and how ignorant I'd been of their high status within
Catholicism. I'd been brought up in the Anglican Church in
New Zealand, a sort of poor
cousin of the Church of
England, and icons were pretty
much entirely missing,
especially those of women.

One of these side chapels at
*Santa Maria* was dedicated to
'Our Lady of Sorrows' which is
one of the titles given to Mary
the Mother, referring to her life
of sorrow. She kind of knocks
your socks off a little when you

first see her. She's actually dressed, which is to say she wears clothes of fabric, not clothes carved into the statue. She's very beautiful. And she looks down at you from an ornate gold and marble alcove. We sat with her for quite a while.

The Santa Maria church was built between 1743 and 1774. It's believed there was a church devoted to Santa Maria on the site previously, it's not known for how long. She was believed to have protected the city in 1688 when lightning set fire to the powder magazine on Mount Urgull behind the basilica and threatened to destroy the whole city. Santa Maria del Coro has been the official patron saint of San Sebastián since 1940.

Notable also was the presence of some stunning modern religious art, on the one hand out of place but on the other hand not. It surprised me to see it in such an old and, I thought, conservative setting, but we continued to see some stunning modern pieces in most of the churches we visited, much to our pleasure.

That night we felt the presence of the Marys watching over us through the night. From various insights and dreams over the previous few days we'd become clear that we were being guided towards drawing together a group of women, most of whom we were already very close to, to form a stronger network of support for each other. That night in San Sebastián we both had a whole load of dreams reinforcing this and Jo in particular understood that we were being very supported by the realms of women saints on high to do the work we were here to do. It wouldn't be the first time we had synchronous dreams of this kind, and we were now starting to get the idea that we were being pulled into the energy of the Marys, and that stumbling upon *Iglesia de Santa Maria* was no accident.

The next morning we stopped by for a coffee at a café in the town. A homeless man outside the café asked if we could buy him a coffee. There were homeless people and beggars most places we went, as there are in so many of the world's large cities now. The difficulty was that we often didn't have any local coins at all, given we generally paid for everything with credit cards. But we were happy to order an extra coffee and Jo took it out to the man. It must have pleased the barista to see it because when we got a second coffee each she didn't charge us.

We were soon on the road again and for the next couple of hours we drove south through the awe-inspiring Basque mountains, impressed with Spanish engineering as we crossed one viaduct after another and drove through multiple tunnels. The day was sunny and the drive was beautiful. Initially we'd intended to drive to Madrid but Jo, looking online again for accommodation, had a brainwave and suggested we stop short of Madrid at a small town we'd never heard of, that apparently had an impressive two-thousand-year-old Roman aqueduct. I love a good ruin so I was all in.

# 4. Segovia, Spain

It seemed a wee bit of a shame to miss Madrid but given it would have been very much a whistle stop, negotiating the centre of such an enormous city late in the day, and then out again early the next morning, it wasn't a bad idea to give it a miss this time round. And as it turned out, Segovia was an inspired choice. Jo's accommodation search came up with a very gorgeous wee spa in the old town; we were always keen on the old parts of towns and did our best to avoid modern hotels, although free wi-fi was always a must, and good parking options were also welcome.

It had been a five or six-hour drive and I was vaguely desperate for a beer. Our hotel turned out to be on the edge of the central plaza which was well-endowed with bars, all with their wicker tables and chairs out in the sun. It was February still but the weather that day was practically sun-bathing conditions. We found a table, ordered two beers (*dos Estrella* – the waiter thought we were asking for *dos Insalada* and tried to find out which sort of salad we wanted), and proceeded to have an hour or so of *I love my life!* in the sunshine, in a beautiful plaza, in Spain. It had been raining and cold for days and days, so it was bliss.

There was a very large church at one end of the plaza and that was our next stop. It was the Segovia Cathedral. It was dedicated to the Virgin Mary. Course it was.

It was built in the 1500s and it's enormous: 105 metres long, 50 wide, with a 90-metre tower (equivalent to 30 stories), earning it the title *The Mother of all Cathedrals*. It replaced an earlier cathedral burnt down in a local uprising. It has a glorious cloister and I love a cloister. I've discovered you can have lots of fun

with light in your photos of cloisters.

It was also very light inside the cathedral, which is just gorgeous. Most cathedrals are very dark but the stone inside Segovia is white and it gives a whole different effect.

One of the side chapels had a stunning icon of Mary (the Mother) in a white gown with a blue veil or cloak – she is generally depicted with a blue cloak and a red or white gown. Next to it is a painting of, we assumed at the time, Mary Magdalene, being crowned by an ascended Jesus, suggesting she was his queen/wife. Mary Magdalene is generally depicted in a red dress with a green cloak or vice versa. It was a radical departure from the official prostitute version though and we were somewhat amazed. Later we realised that it was probably supposed to be Mary the Mother, but the traditional colours

initially fooled us. We liked our idea of it a little more, lending weight to the stories of Mary Magdalene's higher status. She is of course a saint, and did you know she is mentioned in the gospels more than a dozen times, and thus more than most of the apostles? That suggests a station far above the common one most people know of. She is generally depicted with a book, denoting wisdom and her role as a scholar, and an oil jar denoting her role as a healer. The idea that she was a prostitute may have arisen from her red clothing as it's what prostitutes wore at the time (although they also wore yellow); although it's more likely art has mirrored invented life and she was portrayed that way to make that point. Equally her red clothing could indicate status as a religious leader or teacher, or indeed simply to indicate her devotion. She was almost certainly of noble birth and as such very possibly funded Jesus' mission.

Adding to the controversy over her station through the years have been the various New Testament *apocrypha*, or gnostic gospels, writings by early Christians not considered official doctrine by the main branches of the Christian Church. These additional gospels of Mary, Phillip and Thomas, not only place Mary among the apostles, but rank her as the most esteemed, and as speaking on behalf of Jesus. The Gospel of Mary Magdalene, and Mary herself, were held in the highest regard by the Cathars, an unusual Christian sect in the south of France in the middle ages that we were to learn more about.

After roaming the basilica and its very lovely cloister, we wandered through the old town to the castle, which we decided not to go into – it was so vast we didn't really have time to do it justice – and chose instead to head back to the other side of town to the Roman aqueduct. Our timing was impeccable as we caught the late afternoon winter sun with its striking golden glow reflecting off the aqueduct itself. The aqueduct was constructed around 100 AD and runs 15 miles before arriving in the city; at its tallest it's 30 metres (nearly a hundred feet) and has 167 arches where it runs through the city. It's in near perfect condition; it was in continuous operation until the mid-nineteenth century. It *looks* astounding.

We returned to the plaza for dinner – Jo had egg and chips *again* (in her defence, there weren't any other vegetarian options) – and back to our very pretty hotel room where we propped Plastic Jesus up on the telly. He likes it there.

The next day we had a long drive to Fuente Camacho, which is almost to the south coast, and by now I'd figured out that Google Maps calculated time to destination based on the European speed limits of 120-130km/h, which is faster than I tend to drive, so it was going to be a long day. We had a frustrating start with a couple of car complications that included a puncture, forcing me to drive the whole day on the thin spare and thus even slower. (And it was Sunday and no tyre workshops were open.) But we had to be grateful for two lovely Segovian joggers who stopped by to help with tyre changing, even though we had it well in hand. (I say 'we' but in truth it was Jo getting her hands dirty under my car for the second time that morning.) I mean, who would say no, right? We also discovered that a good half of the trip was through what we came to call *boring Spain,* miles and miles of straight roads across flat nothingness, occasionally interspersed with an olive plantation. Eventually that gave way to the amazing mountains of the Andalucía (southern Spain), the Cazorlas and the Nevadas. I really hadn't realised there were so many mountains in Spain, nor how spectacular they were.

# 5. Granada, Spain

For the next 10 days of our house sit in Fuente Camacho it rained. Buckets. And it blew a lot too. *(Come to sunny Spain, they said!)* So there wasn't much getting out, which was fine as we both had work to get on with. We had a brief opportunity to visit Granada though. I'd checked out Google Maps and discovered there was a Mary Magdalene church, so naturally that was top of the list.

We weren't paying much attention to what day of the week it was by this point in our travels, and in fact it was Sunday, so we walked in on mass at the *Iglesia de la Magdalena*. We sat at the back and looked around. It was a stunning church – very old, with clothed statues of the Magdalene, and a replica of Bernadette's grotto in Lourdes built into one wall. A beautiful voice that could have almost been Joan Baez sung a hymn in Spanish, the melody for which was the same as *Blowin' in the Wind*. Apparently Bob Dylan did steal a few things like this. We felt a little conspicuous in the relatively small congregation so we thought we'd go for a wander and come back later when mass was over.

We wandered in the direction of the magnificent Alhambra. In the eighth century, the Iberian peninsula – ie. Spain and Portugal – was conquered by the Muslims of north Africa. They were called Moors, and although they're not especially ethnically different from other Muslim populations they are related to what are still the Berbers of north Africa, particularly Morocco. They were in fairly consistent conflict with Christians from the north and east and were eventually expelled from the region in the late fifteenth century. Their presence in various architecture and ruins remains visible, and none more so than the extraordinary Alhambra of Grenada. It was originally constructed on the remains of a Roman fortress, became the residence of various Emirs and Sultans, and ultimately the royal court of Ferdinand and Isabella.

*The Alhambra[1]*

It's enormous and there was no way we had time to see even a tiny bit of it but we did walk up the hill past its length, enjoying the park setting and the views. A Romani lady stopped Jo and told her fortune. There was quite an involved wee ritual went with it – the woman gave Jo a sprig of rosemary and she had to stamp her feet on the ground twice and pray to Santa Maria. I walked on to avoid being cornered, amusing myself by taking photos of this delightful exchange from a distance.

---

[1] *By Amjad Sheikh https: commons.wikimedia.org w index.php?curid=63826580*

The Alhambra is nearly a kilometre long and covers an area of 35 acres. It's had many mentions in literature and the arts, including Washington Irving's *Tales of the Alhambra*, Salman Rushdie's *The Moor's Last Sigh*, Philippa Gregory's *The Constant Princess*, Paulo Coelho's *The Alchemist*, and the movie and video game *Assassin's Creed.*

Once again though we had animals to get back to – a cat and dog and chickens to feed. Barely a hundred yards from the car though we saw a sign for Grenada Cathedral, and so, you know, why not?! We weren't disappointed; it was loaded with Marys.

As with Segovia, Grenada Cathedral was built with white stone on the inside so it was beautifully light. It has 15 perimeter chapels dedicated to saints, dignitaries and archangels, including *Our Lady of Sorrows*; *Santa Teresa de Avila*; *Santa Ana,* Jesus' grandmother; and *San Miguel Arcangel,* Archangel Michael.

Other chapels also contained statues of Mary the Mother. The icons and statues and pillars and decorations are incredibly ornate, and it's quite overwhelming to be present with such art. There's no doubt that many of them give off auras, and you can see the preference for many among the devoted who light candles at some of the chapels. Mary, of course, is always popular, as is Saint Theresa/Teresa/Therese.

Exit through the gift store and I bought a stunning icon in ancient fashion of Jesus and Mary Magdalene embracing as if they were lovers, with his hand on her breast. Who knew Catholic iconists could be so radical?!

By this time we were clear we were being called, guided, given a talking to, and otherwise blessed by the Marys. We felt we had a responsibility only to follow them – literally geographically – and they would do the rest, filling us with their powerful feminine, healing energy and somehow cleansing us of what we no longer needed. We had nightly visions and dreams of goddesses, women saints, archangels, priestesses and others – sometimes we even had the same dream. One night I saw a woman dressed in purple at the bottom of the bed, 'zapping' me with a beam of white light half the night. I felt sure I'd wake up transformed into Xena. Jo saw a tribe of Avalonian women watching over us, and we both experienced being held in a sphere of light, simultaneously protected and empowered. Jo was emerging from a really challenging time and she felt herself shedding stress layer by layer. I felt myself moving into a new period in my life, less mother, more I'm-not-sure-what. We both had tears at different times, and an immense wonder and gratitude at what seemed a special gift, not only to have this huge experience but also to be sharing it with each other. We laughed *a lot.*

# 6. Málaga, Spain

Málaga is a forty-minute drive due south to the coast from Fuente Camacho and after our house sit ended we headed there for a couple of nights. I was due to fly out of Málaga to Casablanca for a week-long tour of Morocco, and Jo was heading east to Orgiva. Málaga is the main airport for that region and a lot of English people fly in and out of it to their Spanish homes, and rarely do they actually spend time there, but our Camacho hosts had raved about it as their new favourite city so we thought it might be worth a couple of days visit to fill in the gap in our schedules.

There was a cathedral – of course – *Catedral de la Encarnacion de Malaga*, which basically means it's dedicated to Mary the Mother, at the appearance of Gabriel and the incarnation of Jesus. It was a ten-minute walk from our hotel. And the sun was out! It's wonderful to step into the old part of these cities, especially when there's been an obvious amount of care to keep things beautiful and characterful and maintained. Málaga was gorgeous in every way and we had one of our best, most entertaining days here. And there were no pets to hurry home to! When we looked back at the end of our trip and considered which of our cathedral visits we liked best, this was Jo's favourite.

There is a delightful garden of orange trees and palms as you enter the cathedral, giving it a very tropical, kind of 'Californian' feel. In fact there were orange trees everywhere in Málaga and they're lovely to see.

As with the other cathedrals, there were multiple perimeter chapels, and three or four of these were really mind-blowing. The 230-year-old Chapel of the Incarnation, from which the cathedral gets its name, was quite an experience and we were both very drawn to it. A façade of pink marble is overseen by a representation of a third eye in a halo, with multiple white marble or granite statues, representing the Annunciation – the angel Gabriel's appearance before Mary announcing to her that she would conceive and become the mother of Jesus, thus also marking Jesus' incarnation. The central statues are those of Gabriel and Mary. The whole thing is extremely powerful and we sat with it for a long while.

I'd sat down beside Jo and she felt like a massive ball of golden light – it felt as though if I touched her she'd explode. Later Jo said she'd felt she might pass out from the energy 'hit' she got. I'd begun to see Jo had an openness to receiving powerful feminine energy, without even thinking about it or trying. She was naturally some kind of sponge for it and all she had to do was sit there. And then she sends it right back out into the world again, mostly via her music. Jo is basically a pure energy conduit, which is a bloody brilliant thing to be around.

We stayed for ages in Málaga Cathedral, getting 'hits' from the chapels to Raphael, the Sacred Heart, the Magdalene, and Our Lady of Sorrows. Various other art also portrayed Mary and Martha, and Mary Magdalene. Through our music and writing we both knew that we were being guided to shine a Light, and that if we sang and wrote as if we were doing so only to God then miracles would occur.

We eventually headed back out into the sunshine. There is a Picasso museum and art gallery only a block or so from the cathedral so we went there. Picasso was born in Málaga (in 1881) and you can also visit his parents' homes there too. The museum is an incredible collection of his work – a feast, in fact. We stayed a while, in a somewhat vain attempt to take it all in, which is just not possible really. You can *see* it all, but the breadth and depth of his artistic expression is so overwhelming, it would take several visits to absorb it.

Between Picasso and the cathedral, we were feeling emotionally, spiritually, and aesthetically laden and we'd worked up an appetite! In the same wee block there was a row of cafes and we found one with tables in the sun and ordered an enormous seafood paella to share. And a beer. Being a Mary pilgrim can be thirsty work. After days of rain and dog time limits, we were having another *I love my life!* moment. We were even treated to a handsome young Spanish guitar player, who was joined by an older man who'd been trying to catch shoe shine business from patrons a few minutes before morphing into an amazing singer. It was all blissful.

Once we were full of paella and beer, we wandered another few blocks to a Roman amphitheatre and then to the castle rising up behind it. The castle turned out to be quite deceptive. There was a winding path, uphill, that kept looking as though it would lead to an entrance at the next bend. This illusory promise continued around many bends, all the while up a very steep path. There was an amazing view over Málaga's harbour. I was revelling in it and thought it seemed like great exercise; unbeknown to me though, Jo was getting increasingly fraught. At a certain point she stopped suddenly and said she couldn't go on – her fear of heights was getting the better of her. I'd only vaguely understood this was a problem – when we'd visited the aqueduct in Segovia Jo had declined to come up to the top with me, and I knew her flight to Toulouse a few weeks earlier had been a challenge. Now she was in full panic mode, so we quickly turned back. But only a few steps back the other way she thought she'd give it another go. I linked her arm through mine and held her hand tight and up we went. We nearly turned back again several times, but we made it – the path went on for bloody ever – and we were rewarded with a sangria bar at the top! Unexpected bonus! This was the first of a series of height challenges Jo had over the next few weeks, including having to film a video for her next single release high up on the edges of the ruined Moorish castle in Lanjaron the following week. Each time she braved it, more of the fear peeled away. More than once it felt like the Marys were helping push out a fear that no longer served her.

*Up above Málaga at Castillo Gibralfaro*

The castle was gorgeous. Ancient mosaics and beautiful gardens and incredible views of the whole of Málaga; it must have been a seriously luxury stay in its day. You very much get the feeling of an educated society, with a great appreciation for the arts. And of course, Muslim society *was* very advanced in the arts and sciences, more so than the west at many points in history.

After a month together, this was our last evening for a week and we joked about how we'd cope; we both had other adventures to pursue before we'd catch up again. I was excited and a little nervous about visiting Morocco – I'd been wanting to go there for a while. I'd booked a short, small tour that whizzed through some of the highlights of Morocco in a week – the timing had fitted perfectly.

*Sunrise on the Sahara.*

# 7. Montserrat, Spain

Nearly two weeks later, we left Orgiva and Lanjaron in the south of Spain and drove toward the east coast. I'd had an action-packed week in Morocco and Jo had been filming and recording for her new album. I'd even managed to get back to Spain in time for a bit part in her new music video *River.* We were both really tired, and I suppose kind of over-stimulated in a way. There'd been *so much* going on, it was a bit unbelievable. We'd both had a lot of people around and a lot of action and we were ready to just take it quietly for a bit. Our first stop was at a beautiful wee coastal town called Alcossebre. Out of the blue I'd received a very generous invitation from a follower on my Facebook page, and whilst our destination was Montserrat it was too long a drive in one day and Alcossebre was a perfect stop-off point. It was kind of a shame to spend such little time there – it really was an overnight whistle stop and I hope we get to go back again sometime. Our host was lovely, and we felt we'd made a new and very special friend. She told us much of her story over dinner and it wasn't unlike those of amazing women everywhere – powerful and creative and passionate, with a desire for a rich internal life. We managed to laugh and cry our way through so many stories together over dinner, and we were sorry to leave so quickly. We hoped we'd left a little of the Mary energy behind with our host – it seemed as though we had.

Via our social media, our friends were starting to notice that we were on an unexpected pilgrimage and it had been suggested we visit Montserrat, north-west of Madrid. Aside from the fact that it's one of the most striking mountain ranges you'll ever see, Montserrat is famous for its monastery way up high in its rocky peaks, which in turn is famous for its *Black Madonna,* a statue of a black-skinned Mary and child. This was going to be a day and a half – it felt like five adventures packed into one day.

For a start it was the thirty-fifth anniversary of my mother's death. She died when I was only twenty and it had been, and remains, the biggest gut-wrench of my life. She was forty-six. I was now nearly a decade older than her. It was also the first anniversary of her death since my father passed nine months previously. It all felt pretty momentous.

We drove up from Alcossebre to Montserrat. As we skirted Barcelona and headed inland we could see Montserrat looming in the distance. It's a rocky mountain range – it reminds me a little of New Zealand's Remarkables range along Lake Wakitipu in the South Island, albeit that it's far more jagged. 'Montserrat' literally means 'serrated mountain' – it looks like a saw. The further we got into it, the more it looked like a mountain of ancient standing stones. Every narrow bend we rounded revealed a concourse of rocky beings looming above us. It's a spectacular drive.

It was surprisingly busy at the top for the time of year, but we rather cannily found a park. It had been snowing and was very cold, but the sun was out. We grabbed a coffee – much needed – and walked up the road to the monastery buildings. There's a sheer drop from part of the road, with a huge vista across to the Pyrenees in the distance. Jo was on high alert, although determined to walk that bit of road nonetheless. She even did a 'Facebook Live' recording standing there. In fact we did live recordings simultaneously, such was our desire to share the mere fact that we were there in that amazing place.

The monastery was founded in the 11th century and still functions, with over 70 monks. The buildings are beautiful, and so stunning with the rocky Montserrat rising above them.

After going the wrong way through the tourist system – typical – we found our way to the basilica. It's smaller than most we'd been in, but equally spectacular for its ornamentation. As with others there were a series of side chapels and I was especially drawn to that of Saint Scholastica – not that I knew it was her – we thought at the time

it was Saint Therese. My tiredness and emotions overcame me here and I had a small flood of uncontrollable tears. Or a large one, depending on how you rate these things. The statue of Scholastica did seem especially benevolent and loving, looking down at us from some height. She was the sister of Saint Benedict (possibly his twin), and Montserrat is a Benedictine centre. She was born in Umbria around 480 to wealthy parents; she is the patron saint of nuns and education.

After I'd recovered myself we walked back around to the other side of the church where we could enter the walkway to visit the

famous *Black Madonna.* She sits in a highly protected alcove visible high above the main altar, and it's quite an interesting walk around and up to see her. The stairs on the way up are decorated with portraits of the women saints, and there are 'custodians' carved into the metal doors to her alcove. There's only room for a slow single file of pilgrims to walk past her, so I can imagine it's a long wait in the high season – we didn't wait long. The Madonna and Child are surrounded by protective perspex but the globe in her right hand passes through the perspex so pilgrims can touch it. After filing past, and down the other side, you can visit the *Sala del Cambril*, a small circular chapel. It's a very beautiful, peaceful space for quiet meditation, interrupted only occasionally by Chinese tourists with selfie sticks who sadly don't take the time to sit and reflect.

For me, this was the most profound of our pilgrimages; not because I was touched especially by the Madonna here (not so much as others we'd come across), but I think mainly because of the location and the importance of the date. I think there's something about being in mountains that brings you symbolically closer to the people you've loved and now miss. I was in the Himalayas when my father died and it seemed a perfect place to be. Montserrat, the mountains, are incredibly moving, and although nowhere near as high as the Himalayas, equally as striking for their unusual formations. However, we had a very long drive ahead of us, north to the Pyrenees and across to France, so sadly we couldn't stay longer. But by no means were our adventures done for the day; the drive through the Spanish side of the Pyrenees was fabulous. The day was still sunny and it was very scenic. Through one very long five-kilometre tunnel you enter out onto something of an alpine plateau, and past small towns through one of which is the border. Into the French side the temperature dropped and we were in literally mountains of snow. It looked like Narnia! I was slightly wary of the state of the roads and I was starting to tire – for some reason I hadn't slept much the previous two nights, but we kept on – the last hour or two seemed to take forever and it was dark by the time we reached the very tiny, very old village of Sougraigne where we would stay the night. There was snow, it was freezing, our wee hotel creaked, and it was probably just a little bit haunted. I was very pleased to be horizontal. We'd bought goat's cheese and fig cake in Montserrat, which we ate with bread and salad and our usual dose of gin. The next day was going to be a serious Magdalene day.

*Through snowy deserted villages in the Pyrenees, to our not-at-all-likely-to-be haunted B&B.*

# 8. Rennes-le-Château, France

We were keeping a very tight schedule during this week, and trying to fit in as much as we could before catching the ferry back to England that had been booked weeks before, and squeezing in time to visit my cousin (also called Sue Fitzmaurice), in the Bordeaux. Rennes-le-Château was a priority.

Rennes-le-Château is a small French hilltop village populated since at least 500 AD. For many years, Rennes-le-Château has been the subject of various theories (and conspiracy theories) about Mary Magdalene's travels to France, the remains of Christ, the Holy Grail, and similar. Considerable renown has grown out of Dan Brown's *The Da Vinci Code,* which itself drew from *The Holy Blood and the Holy Grail,* a book by Michael Baigent, Richard Leigh and Henry Lincoln; and from other writers including Jules Verne. Much of the conspiracy derives from a former priest of the village church, Bérenger Saunière, and suggestions of hidden treasures and various characters having gone to their graves bearing secrets. Other theories grew from the assertion that the Merovingian line of French kings that ruled from the 5th to the 9th centuries was descended from Jesus and the child he had with Mary Magdalene. None of this is proven, and much of it is scoffed at by historians. Nonetheless, the village church is dedicated to

Mary Magdalene, and there has been a church on this site since at least the 9th century.

How this wee village, with a population of a hundred or so, handles its tens of thousands of visitors during the tourist season I can't imagine. Not for the first time we were thrilled to be visiting out of season. The Church is one of the sweetest, and certainly the most feminine, I've ever seen. The interior is soft pink and yellow and blue, and the icons are similarly coordinated. That perhaps makes it sound a little lollypop'ish, but it's not at all.

Mary Magdalene makes two appearances, once at the side of the nave, and once behind the altar where she holds a child, daringly suggested to be Jesus' child. Mary is most often portrayed with a book and an urn or jug of oil, demonstrating knowledge and healing. Unusually here she is dressed in gold. In the icon at the altar, she is in her more typical red gown with green cloak.

Jesus stands opposite her, also carrying a child. Were there twins? The idea that Mary Magdalene escaped persecution in the holy land, landing in the south of France, isn't entirely fanciful and is very popular among more than just conspiracy theorists. That Mary may have been Jesus' wife, seems possible. That she was foremost among his apostles, I find very likely. That she was a prostitute was a shameful fabrication designed to diminish the power of women.

Students of religion and mythology will understand the connection between myth and how various figures in religion have been portrayed with the same characteristics. For instance, there are many parallels to be drawn between Jesus and Horus[2], the god of the sky. The story of sisters Sekhmet and Hathor has parallels to the two Marys. Jo explained it to me, along with the connections that can be derived. It's an interesting lesson.

Sekhmet and Hathor were believed to be the daughters of the Sun God Ra. Both were born from the rather unsettling act of him pulling his eyes out, hence they are the 'eyes of god'. Sekhmet is the lion-headed goddess of justice and fierceness. Portrayed usually as a sensual, naked, unashamed warrior she represents a part of all of us that is instinctual and courageous, that knows what's right and wrong. She is powerful. Hathor her twin sister has the head of a cow and is the mother: peaceful, gentle, loving and all embracing. Ra said one could not live without the other, and as such we have to embrace both sets of characteristics in life. These symbols of womanhood/ goddess figures have carried down through the pantheons of India, Rome and Greece and can be seen in all of mythology. Mary the Mother has the characteristics of Hathor; Mary Magdalene those of Sekhmet. And so together the two Marys embody both essential parts of being a balanced whole woman. To be soft without passion, or vice versa, is to be out of balance.

---

[2] Both births celebrated on 25th December, both said to have 3 wise men attend their births, both had 12 disciples, both performed miracles, both crucified and resurrected.

Sekhmet and Hathor are portrayed with similar colours to the Marys; and Mother Mary is often portrayed with a crescent moon beneath her feet, reminiscent of cow horns.

Sekhmet and Hathor were going to come up again for us in our accidental pilgrimage, as the energy of the Marys continued to unfold for us.

*Jo at Rennes-le-Chateau with the Magdalene Tower to the right and the Pyrenees left.*

Despite our frequent sarcasm about the *Exit Through the Gift Shop*, we were total suckers for them. We sometimes even went to the gift shop first! There was a lot that was tacky and we did still have a contest for who could find the best Katholic Kitsch; but there was also beautiful jewellery, hand-painted icons, various original art, and so on. We both had wee collections already, most particularly bracelets with small charms of saints and symbols. Of course, we had the Marys; and we had both acquired Rita. I'd started my collection with Bernadette. For two non-Catholics, well… it wasn't obvious. By the time our accidental pilgrimage ended I had five of these and was delighted to gift two of them when I returned briefly to New Zealand, one to my son to remind him how much I loved him. He's a chef and I said it was fine if it got greasy and grimy since sometimes love could get a bit that way.

At Rennes-le-Château though we were frustrated by the shop's eftpos machine not working on any of the cards we had on us, although we scraped up a few euros between us to get the bracelets we wanted most of all. What we hadn't realised was that the museum entry (for which there was a fee) was also the entry to the orangery and the Magdalene Tower. By the time we woke up to this we had €7.50 in coins between us and we needed €9.50. We knew we had a good €10 or more in change in the car but that would mean walking all the way back to the car park in the freezing cold. I appealed to the shop assistant to allow us both through anyway but she wasn't having it, so I insisted Jo went. I stayed in the shop and managed to avoid scowling at the shop assistant.

About twenty minutes later, Jo emerged. As it turned out the tower was on the edge of a precipice and she'd made it to the top, on her own, alone and unaided, with wind and windows rattling all around her in the howling cold weather. She'd even managed a short video with full tower and weather sound effects. Not haunted at all.

*Da Vinci Code* fans and holy grail seekers believe the codes to Mary Magdalene are in the tower. Jo had wanted to see what they were. It was a library of red leather-bound books, so another item added to our *To Do* list, to go back and read those one day. The priest, Saunière, source of much of the conspiracy (and for whom Louvre curator and Priory of Sion grand master Jacques Saunière in *The Da Vinci Code* is named), is somewhat eerily buried in the tower yard, in the midst of his own rather obsessive creation.

From all sides of the village there are incredible views out over valleys and other mountains, with the Pyrenees to the south still looming large. A rocky outcrop a mile away has caves that supposedly were home to a fugitive Mary Magdalene. They would have to wait for another day too. By now we were freezing. I smiled at the shop assistant and we headed back to our car.

# 9. Montségur, France

Montségur is a small town famous for its castle, the Chateau de Montségur, that was built on the ruins of the last stronghold of the Cathars.

The Cathars were a Christian sect during the Middle Ages, with a belief that placed Mary Magdalene in a much more central role than the traditional Church of the day. They were considered heretical by the Catholic Church which had been trying to destroy the sect for decades. Towards the end of this period, 10,000 French troops lay siege to the fortress and after nine months its 500 inhabitants surrendered. Over 200 Cathars were burnt to death in a mass bonfire at the foot of the mountain. Prior to the fall of the fortress, several Cathars supposedly escaped with a mysterious treasure, variously speculated to be the treasury, esoteric books or even the actual Holy Grail. The names of many of the victims are remembered every year on the anniversary of the massacre on 16 March.

Cathars viewed women as equal believers to men, viewing the soul as without gender. As such, they saw women as being equally capable as leaders. They gave more importance to the role of Mary Magdalene as a teacher and in the spread of early Christianity, possibly viewing her with more importance even than Saint Peter, the founder of the Church.

It was a beautiful drive from Rennes-le-Chateau to Montségur, through mountains and gorges, over rivers and through valleys, past several pretty and sleepy villages. When Montsegur came into view, our first thoughts were *How on earth do you get up there?!* We'd heard we could drive quite close but looking at it from afar that just seemed an impossibility. We weren't sure we'd have time to walk it.

The mountain seems like solid rock and the fortress atop it is massive and grey and fierce. How it was even built in the first-place beggars belief. Just the zig-zag drive up the side set Jo on edge. It felt dark and foreboding and it seemed there were ghosts of violent oppression here. I was struck by a memory of this place, as was Jo. It was sad but deeply powerful and I knew it was a place of connection for us.

Time prevented us from staying. I don't think I could have climbed the mountain that day even if we'd had time – there was a heaviness to it that I didn't want to stay with just then. We *will* go back though, and we *will* climb to the top.

We had several hours more to journey still, to my cousin's villa in the Bordeaux; a pilgrimage and respite of a different sort. My cousin and I share the same name, and due to uncannily strong genes (we're sixth cousins) we're also remarkably similar both in appearance and personality traits. We enjoyed a blissful couple of days, mostly doing not very much at all, except for a quick visit to the lovely and very old town of *Saint-Émilion*, which itself has a very old and beautiful cathedral. There was building work going on when we popped in and all the icons were covered with dark brown drapes. There was supposedly an icon of Joan of Arc and we amused ourselves looking up the drapes trying to find her. Didn't seem at all the right kind of behaviour for a cathedral.

It was a god-send to not have to drive for a day; we'd had three long driving days back-to-back and I was exhausted from it.

*Some stunning modern art gracing the walls of the cloister at the Cathedral of Saint-Émilion*

# 10. Chartres, France

Chartres had been on our list from very early on. Jo had visited before and had a good friend who was a guide there six months of the year who had recommended very strongly that we go. Sadly she wasn't there herself at the time. I'd vaguely checked out accommodation options and thought the old Benedictine monastery – now a hotel – looked ideal. Jo had also found the same option independently and her friend had emailed with the same recommendation, so that was a definite then.

We drove through several diverse parts of French countryside towards the north. It was misty and Devon'ish much of the way. We took a peculiar detour of our own devising, via a wee town called Pazayac. I'd dreamt we'd been girls in a French town called Paz and it was the only town with a name starting with that spelling so we thought *Why not.* Pazayac was tiny; we walked around a little, especially enamoured of the church bells that rang rather a lot in the brief time we were there. It seemed familiar and it seemed to want to tell us something but we couldn't quite hear it. Possibly it was *Don't be ridiculous* but we were relaxed and happy to indulge our dreams in this way.

We visited a small cemetery that held only family crypts, some of which looked like glasshouses. It was so unusual. A nearby, slightly dapper, scarecrow completed this very Henry James scene.

Prior to Chartres, the countryside levels out into a great flat nothingness that doesn't seem as though it could possibly give rise to one of the world's greatest cathedrals, but yet eventually it did. We checked into our monastic hotel – our room was pretty cell-like. The shower was so small you pretty much had to climb in on your hands and knees in a prayer position, and the window was so high up you could only see out by climbing – and standing – on the windowsill.

We went across to the cathedral. It was evening already but we

 were keen to get there and walk the huge labyrinth in the cathedral nave, since it was cleared of chairs only on a Friday. Our hotel was barely a hundred metres away and rounding the corner of the alleyway into the cathedral forecourt is a *Wow!* experience.

I felt like I was being sucked in across the forecourt and inside, such was the pull it seemed to have. Sadly, although it was Friday, it wasn't chair-less. Another *to-do* for the future. We'd seen already, from the high window in our cell/room, that there were two other labyrinths nearby, so we hoped to locate the entry to these at some point.

Jo pretty much made a bee-line for a particular chapel where an icon of a gold-draped Madonna and Child stood. I'd really come to love these small side chapels in the cathedrals. Each had its own art and history and story and feeling. I walked the nave and visited the central chapel and altar before joining Jo at the chapel of Our Lady of Chartres, sitting across from her. I figured she knew the best spots to sit and reflect, so I was all over being led.

This beautiful Madonna was commissioned in 1508 and given to the church in 1540, whereupon she lived beneath the church in the crypt. She was placed on her pillar in 1806, prior to which she was known as "the Black Virgin". Like many others, she had turned dark after years of candles being burnt before her in supplication. Legend has it that a site of druid pagan worship existed here long before the first church (the current cathedral is the fifth church on the site and dates from around 1200) and that there were beliefs among this group, *pre-Christianity,* that a virgin would bring forth a child of God. A predecessor to the current Madonna had supposedly been worshipped in what are now the crypts beneath Chartres.

When I sat in Her chapel, there was a powerful golden air about and an almost blinding gold energy coming from the Madonna herself. I could see a solid three or four-inch beam of it going straight into Jo. I knew if I was sitting right next to her I'd feel it coming off her. It seemed to me as though the Marys looked around for whoever was the best vessel for their power and that's where they aimed. Jo says I got just as much as her and it only seems that way. With all of this powerful Mary energy we were soaking up though, it did have the effect of pushing things out in both of us, so we often had moments of feeling physically or emotionally off in various ways, but we also very much saw this as a good thing. The Marys were deciding what no longer served us and out it went.

I think to all outward appearances it looked as though we were just having a light-hearted holiday, but the truth was we were both working as we went – Jo was working extremely hard, primarily on the PR schedule for the release of her upcoming album *An Abandoned Orchid House*[3], as well as writing and recording music – *and* we were both dealing with our own internal changes. It wasn't always a picnic. I was amazed at what went into PR for the album – it was massive, and involved a lot of phone calls, emails, art work, oversight of various aspects of final production, finding all kinds of best deals for printing this, that and the other thing. Songs had to have codes for this and codes for that, and digital codes needed to embed different people's copyrights, and all kinds of other rights, and royalties, and yada yada. It was intense; really intense.

I'd listened to Jo's music, including the new album, and had sat in the same room as she composed; I recognised and appreciated her talent by now and what she was trying to achieve and I wanted more than anything for her to succeed. For whatever reason, the gods had thrown us together on this strange and whacky journey at this time and we had come to view it as some kind of privilege and gift.

---

[3] Under her stage name *Talitha Rise.*

We took it easy the next day, enjoying our monastic cell picnic of salad, biscuits, cheese and crackers, and yes, gin. We wandered over to the cathedral in the afternoon. This time we could enjoy the light through the cathedral's magnificent stained glass as well. The previous evening we'd also sat at the chapel of the *Sancta Camisa* – the Virgin's Veil. We hadn't really got the same 'hit' from it the night before, but this time it was

offering a lot. A glass case houses a barely visible cloth behind a locked cast iron grate. It is believed to be variously the veil of Mother Mary or the tunic she wore when she gave birth to Jesus. Supposedly carbon dating places it in the first century and it is of the style of the region. Church legend states it was gifted to Charlemagne in the ninth century from the Empress of Byzantium.

We both received messages here that were very similar and we talked about them as we walked a little through the old town.

Mine was that you had to transmit whatever it was that you were here to transmit, and it didn't matter what that was since at its core it was all love anyway.

Jo's was that we had to let love inhabit us, rather than trying to inhabit love out there somewhere.

The wee old town around the Cathedral is lovely. Full of pretty cafes, shops, restaurants, and delis. We were being careful what we ate otherwise we would have properly indulged via the many pastry and sweet shops!

Later we found our way to a grassy labyrinth next to the Cathedral. It's beautifully meditative to walk.

Again, there was so much here that we didn't have time to see, not to mention we were both really tired. A tour of the crypt will be a future definite, and more time enjoying the gorgeous old town around the cathedral.

# 11. Rouen, France

It was Palm Sunday when we drove through Rouen en route to our ferry from Caen to Portsmouth. We'd been tossing up whether to go to Mont St Michel – we really wanted to – but we couldn't do both and Rouen won out. Naturally the cathedral was dedicated to Our Lady. And I was keen to also visit the nearby *Eglise de Jeanne d'Arc* – the Church of Joan of Arc. Jo had visited the Church of Joan of Arc on a school trip when she was 11 – when she saw it again she thought it had got a lot smaller.

We arrived at the Cathedral during mass – everyone was holding sprigs of greenery that you could smell all through the church. There were some exquisite choir voices, but we didn't have long so we headed towards the other church. We'd also wanted to visit the Jeanne d'Arc museum but it had a set guided tour that we didn't have time for. The future *To Do* list was getting quite long.

Joan of Arc was a French peasant girl who claimed to have had visions of St Michael, St Catherine and St Margaret in her father's garden in 1425. Three years later she claimed that the French would only defeat the English in the latter's occupation of northern France if she were at the head of the French army. Various predictions she made came true, leading the French

Dauphin to acquiesce to her request. She was captured by the English three years later, tried, and burnt at the stake. She was 19 years old.

Her Church in Rouen is built next to the ruins of the former Church of St Vincent which was destroyed in World War II. It's a tragic spot in many ways – when I posted a picture of the square on my Facebook page a friend commented that his great uncle was shot there, by Nazis during World War II. It's also the site of Joan's execution.

The modern church has an unusual architecture. In some ways I found it difficult to see it as attractive, at least from the outside, after visiting so many ancient places in recent weeks – it's a little awkward and at odds with its surroundings – one imagines locals were probably not thrilled with the design. The feeling changes once you're inside though. It's open and light in a way you don't see at all in older churches. And its stained glass is taken from the original church. There is an undoubted femininity to the semi-circular space that draws little divide between congregation and altar. A gold statue of Joan – modern and beautiful – stands at the rear of the congregation, her arms in a humble welcome.

Joan has no burial site; her body was burned twice more following her death and her ashes were thrown into the Seine to prevent the collection of relics. In 1456, a Papal court examined the trial, pronounced her innocent, and declared her a martyr. In 1803 she was declared a national symbol of France by Napoleon Bonaparte. She was beatified in 1909 and canonised in 1920 and is one of nine secondary patron saints of France.

We returned to the main cathedral, which by now had glorious loud bells ringing out. We found less inside that drew us in however and we did not stay long. Perhaps we should have gone to Mont St Michel after all, although it felt special to visit *Eglise de Jeanne d'Arc.*

We headed north-west to Caen for our ferry – it was going to be another long day – a five-hour crossing over the Channel, and then a drive up to North London, where fortunately my good friend and London host, a night owl, would still be up. The channel crossing was smooth and we variously dozed and wandered a little on the very windy deck. We were a little sad to be leaving the continent.

# 12. Glastonbury, England

After ten days in Manchester, dog-sitting, writing, recording... we had a few days before I had to fly home to New Zealand and Australia for several weeks, and we needed to head south, so we spontaneously decided – it's always 'accidental' – to spend a few days in Glastonbury. It's a place loaded with the energy of the Marys and seemed the perfect finishing spot. Friends of Jo's ran a lovely B&B a block back from town – they're *always* fully booked but surprisingly they weren't on the few days we planned on being there. It's called *Pilgrims,* and all their rooms are named after goddesses. We got *Magdalene.* You can't make this stuff up!

It was an interesting drive, moving away from the heavier energy of the north and into the lighter energy of the south, and the even lighter energy of Somerset, around Glastonbury. It had been mizzle all the way south but started to clear as we entered the county. After off-loading our things into our room, we went out in search of food and drink and ended up at the characterful *Who'd A Thought It* pub. We slept incredibly peacefully. Which was a good thing as the next two days were pretty much the whole Glastonbury experience, and you really can't do that whole thing without having some emotional responses. And we did.

We started the next day with a fantastic breakfast at *Pilgrims* (best bacon ever – although they cater to every dietary requirement known to man), and without wasting much time we went on to have chocolate Guinness cake at Heaphy's cafe. Which was definitely *to live for*.

We visited some of the gorgeous shops along the main road, and then went to the Goddess Temple. To understand Glastonbury, you have to understand its history, mythical or otherwise, and its dedication to the goddess movement.

Glastonbury is dominated by the Tor (which just means hill, but some hills are Tors and some are just hills), with the remains of St Michael's Church atop it. It's said to be the original Avalon. It lies at the centre of the Mary and Michael ley lines and is considered a sacred and living thing. It's also one of the Earth's identified chakras, namely the 4th heart chakra, so it's a powerful place.

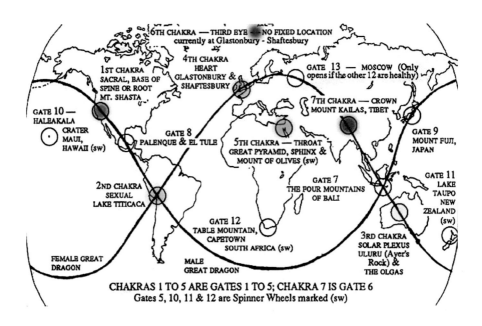

CHAKRAS 1 TO 5 ARE GATES 1 TO 5; CHAKRA 7 IS GATE 6
Gates 5, 10, 11 & 12 are Spinner Wheels marked (sw)

Avalon was a feminine society that worshiped both the individual goddesses and the one Goddess. It lived in a sacred relationship with the land, which it respected and treated with care. Glastonbury was previously known as the Isle of Avalon and there is considerable desire to return the town to that name. The adoration of the Goddess by inhabitants of the area has never entirely waned and its resurgence has made Glastonbury an international – arguably *the* international – centre of goddess faith.

The Goddess Temple was opened in 2002. Priestess training has taken place there ever since; and the temple, the Goddess Hall (pictured) and Goddess House are all run by a team of women – and men – priestesses, priests and volunteers. Its influence in the area is undeniable.

So when the Temple opened at noon we were excited to visit. Jo had been many times previously, having visited often over the previous twenty years, as well as having lived in Glastonbury for a time. I'd previously visited Glastonbury only once briefly, had walked up the Tor on a beautiful summer evening and had cider and pie at *The George and Pilgrims*.

The Temple changes its interior a little depending on the season and whether there are any particular goddess days to celebrate. We were there during Spring Equinox where they celebrate the Goddess Ostara (Easter as she became in Christianity), although the music that day was all Bridget-themed, which was funny as we'd been talking about Ireland a lot. The Temple is a place of quiet reflection for the most part. It's warm, comfortable, peaceful, and loving. It

96

embraces you and accepts whatever you have to offer, happy to reflect back to you whatever it thinks you need. We sat a while, we both had tears, and Jo accepted a smudge cleanse from the volunteer guide (known as a Melissa) seated there. We knew, having travelled to so many places of pilgrimage the previous several weeks, that the Goddess was not only going to accept us as pilgrims, She would very definitely evoke significant cleansing and change. I suppose for the most part we hoped that would be peaceful, but in hindsight that may have been too much to expect.

We emerged back out into the cool English drizzle and walked. I was being led by Jo, and Jo was being internally guided as to where to next, which was in the direction of the Tor.

We were both accelerating through ups and downs and could feel 'stuff' – emotional baggage – just sloughing off almost constantly; we pretty much just went with it. We both had so much insight during this time, for ourselves and each other, into our own spiritual growth and the nature of womanhood. The Marys were helping us, and their story and its intricacies were profound.

We walked towards the White Well, at the foot of the Tor. It wasn't quite open yet and we wandered up the road to the Tor, stopping short at a farm gate where some sheep wandered over to us. We weren't quite ready for the Tor. *It doesn't always want you,* Jo said. Rumour has it that if you walk up the Tor angry or moody, the Tor will throw you off. We meandered back to the White Well, an outlet of a pure underground stream from the Tor, manned each day – womanned actually – by volunteers who light candles and bring offerings into an unusual and very dark shrine of sorts, hued from the stone and a brick surround. It was very obviously a sacred space, dominated by the sound of water moving rapidly through stone in an enclosed space, loud but reassuring in its own way. We walked in the direction of the path up the Tor, and by the time we got there it was ready for us.

As we climbed the muddy steps, Jo became her storyteller self and recounted the story of Ra's creation of Sekhmet and Hathor – his daughters – why he created them and the things they did. It's a very sacred story and has to be told verbally so I won't recount it here.

The point of telling the story is to consider which part of it you resonate with and why. For me at that time it was the birth/creation of Hathor. I know next time I hear the story it will be another part. And the time after that. Jo promised a second part to the story when I was ready.

There were only a few people at the top of the Tor when we reached it. We circled around in our own directions and with our own thoughts.

Walking down, we talked about Sekhmet and Hathor, and the two Marys, and how they were all related, and which we each identified with more and which we wanted to balance with more. We both had both elements within us, as did all women, but which was where and which was ready to emerge more strongly were the questions on our minds. We both felt we were birthing new selves – a culmination of our two-month pilgrimage and the Marys working away on us, both with and without our knowledge.

As we walked back to town, we passed a shop window that called out (not in any metaphysical sense – we were just overcome with a desire for a retail experience) and we crossed the road to find a treasure trove of funky and very original clothes, which to be fair there are a lot of in Glastonbury. We played dress-up for an hour or so with the delightful owner, Pink Anne, and Jo bought an upcycled Afghan coat to replace a beloved former relic that had sadly passed to the big second-hand store in the sky the previous year. That meant there was an opening for the long black coat she'd been wearing since we returned to England two weeks previously and I felt my sensible outdoor country dog-walking coat wasn't quite cutting it in Glastonbury so I claimed the black coat before it went the way of the old Afghan. It was time for *The George & Pilgrims.*

Here Jo recited the second part of the story, to do with the phases we pass through as girls and women, and the cycling through our emerging selves, our Sekhmet and Hathor.

All women go through all stages; it's just when and how. I knew exactly where I was at, and I also knew it had been pressing on me for some time. In fact we were both there in our own ways – I needed to develop more of Hathor on the outside as my Sekhmet was ever-present); and Jo needed to develop her Sekhmet on the inside as her Hathor was ever present on the outside. Of course, it also wasn't quite that cut and dried either, as we're both of us already soft on the outside and strong on the inside in our own ways. But there was a new upward spiral coming.

*Cod Almighty* was our name for the fish dinners we had at *The George & Pilgrims* – a delicious feast, accompanied by gin and Guinness respectively. I've tried to like Guinness, I really have. It's more of a food than a drink. Apparently I need to put more effort into it. Fortunately we didn't have far to go to our B&B. We weren't long back though and I suddenly dropped into a black hole of mood – a bit of the black dog – very unexpected as it had been a long time since that particular bitch had paid a visit. I knew it was a cleaning-out of sorts; I cried – actually, I sobbed. There was no particular focus for my sadness and blackness – it was a bit of both (if you've had the blackness, you'll know it's quite different from sadness), but I also knew in the back of my mind that this part of our journey was about to come to an end and I was really starting to grieve a little over that. After a while my mood lifted almost as quickly as it had arrived. We were on a bit of rollercoaster, but we were both experienced enough to know it, and knowledgeable enough to know how to handle it. In that particular moment, a hug and a cup of tea went down a treat.

That night we both had loads of dreams. I kept waking up in a hot flash, exhausted, and then let go of whatever frenzy took hold of my mind, focused on the Goddess' purple cloak enfolding us, and went back to sleep for the next round. I lost count of how many rounds there were.

In one of my more hilarious dreams, I found myself the leader of a minor political party. I'd gone up to a journalist to ask if he'd like my opinion on something and he'd responded *No, I don't need your opinion.* Just then, Nicola Sturgeon, the leader of Scotland's SNP and the country's First Minister, walked in and was very palsy with me in front of the male journalist. Then the conservative women leaders walked past us and on up a hallway, and with our arms around each other, Nicola and I opened the door to the hallway and I yelled *You're just jealous because we're prettier than you!* When I recounted it to Jo the next morning I just about fell off my bed laughing.

In another dream, Jo and I were walking into our medieval-type village after visiting another village where there was a rainbow goddess temple. We'd decided there was room in the world for another goddess temple and we were all about building a purple one.

All my dreams that night had a pall of purple across them.

We headed off into town again the next morning, visiting *Gecko Café* – another of Glastonbury's finest – for coffee. It was market day and there were some funky clothing stalls out. I'd resolved not to buy myself gifts in Glastonbury, not least since there was no end to what I *could* very happily part with my money for, but also because every time I saw something beautiful I clearly got the message that I wasn't there to buy things – I was there to soak up the energy of Glastonbury. However, in one fast swoop I did buy a couple of deliciously purple, gorgeously witchy things. And a silver rose ring, a symbol of Mother Mary.

A little further on is St Mary's Church and the Magdalene Chapel. Actually, technically it's St Margaret's Chapel and the Magdalene alms houses – the latter are no longer in use and it's believed the former had originally been called the Magdalene Chapel anyway, changing its name to some more politically correct saint. Saint Margaret had been Queen Margaret of Scotland. She was an English princess (1045-1093) and had fled to Scotland following the Norman Conquest and married Malcolm III of Scotland, becoming Queen of Scots. She's sometimes called The Pearl of Scotland.

There is a dozen or so Queen Margaret or Saint Margaret girls' schools around the world – my daughter had attended the one in Wellington, New Zealand. And being of Scottish heritage ourselves also, she has a certain place in our lives.

Just inside this lovely wee chapel are two icon paintings, one each of Mary Magdalene and Saint Margaret. They were painted by John Coleman, an official iconographer for the Anglican Church. Jo had studied with John for several months in 2012, and the icon of Saint Margaret was her design, officially approved as the Saint Margaret icon by the Anglican Church. She wears regal purple and red robes, embossed with her official coat of arms which itself is not unlike the Scottish Cross of Saint Andrew. She has a crown and carries a model of the chapel in one hand and a thistle in the other. Both paintings are striking.

We lit a candle at both icons and sat a while in what was a *very* sensual energy, almost electric. This was the Magdalene. Wow! We returned to the Goddess Temple. It already felt like coming home. A great purple, horned goddess statue stood next to where I sat down and I felt a powerful, earthy energy infuse through me. In goddess myth and culture, horns are signs of the life-giving cow and the Earth Mother; of nature, fertility and abundance. I felt a new power rising within me and I was very at peace.

There were sets of angel and goddess cards around and we each took a different set to make a card selection. I drew Sekhmet. And then because I tend towards greed I drew a second. Sekhmet again. I checked to make sure they weren't all Sekhmet. Nope.

I know the Temple will be a place I'll return to again many times.

We went on to visit Chalice Well, site of a magical underground stream, beautiful gardens, and a retreat centre. That evening it was The George & Pilgrims *again*, but we were really worn out and didn't stay long.

That night my dreams exhausted me and I woke up shattered and tearful, which was pretty much how I was for the rest of the day, at times crying uncontrollably. I felt like I was about to lose an arm. Two months of magic was coming to an end. Except we also both knew it was really just a beginning. I'm not someone who cries with goodbyes – the only time I remember doing so was just before putting my sixteen-year-old on a plane to South America on her own three years before. But on this occasion now, I was very tired, and feeling full of some energy or other about to burst out and birth some new me. I could honestly say I wasn't myself. It's an unusual experience to spend twenty-four hours a day with someone, seven days a week, for two months, who you only just met. I would not have imagined it possible. And yet that's precisely what we had done, and there hadn't been a single dull moment, nor a cross word – not so much as a mild irritation even. It was an incredible 'accidental' journey; the company made it magic.

After breakfast I re-arranged my luggage for six weeks in New Zealand and Australia – it would be cooler in New Zealand and still warm in Western Australia, which meant a mixture of clothes to pack. When I came back at the end of May I'd have only a few days turnaround in London before heading to Greece – I tried to make sense of everything in my car so I'd be able to swap clothes again when I got back. We'd nicknamed my car *Shirley Valentine* – she was a suburban girl from Scotland who'd been on a big adventure to Europe. She'd done well.

We said goodbye to Brian and Clare at *Pilgrims* – we knew we'd be back.

# Epilogue

I can't recall precisely at what point I decided to write this book – somewhere between Montserrat and Chartres I think. At any rate, our visit to Glastonbury was thought up and happened after the book was already half written. When you start writing a book you don't always know how it's going to end – you hope you'll find some appropriate ending, where characters and plot reach some elegant conclusion. Not only did Glastonbury close the circle of the journey – at least spiritually, if not especially geographically – it made some new sense of everything that came before it.

To begin with we didn't even know we were *on* a pilgrimage – it took at least to Segovia to realise it. Then it became about soaking up the energy of the Marys. Glastonbury spelled out to us what soaking up that energy was really all about.

I've had some fabulous adventures in my life – I've rafted the Grand Canyon; I took my daughter out of school for a year when she was 14-15 and we travelled the world; my first trip to Ireland and Scotland was memorable; India has been profound – twice; I've visited the Holy Land on a pilgrimage to the Baha'i World Centre; and others. I'd be hard-pushed to put these in any order but if I did then arguably the *Accidental Mary Pilgrimage* would come first.

I'm middle-aged and my children have grown up. I left home two years ago, knowing there was more to see and to learn and that this was a new and exciting era of potentiality for me. My spiritual development and purpose have been at the core of that journey, and I've been blessed to have met so many gorgeous, wonderful people along the way, and to have had numerous experiences that have influenced me at the core. Despite all that's been amazing through those two years, I knew there was a turning point coming – a more refined heart journey, of creativity in particular. I had no idea two Marys and a Jo would turn up to go with me.

As I complete this book, I've been back in New Zealand for three weeks, and as I chat daily with Jo in England, the Marys are still toying with both of us, pushing us, helping us, ever present, as I'm sure they will remain. We're grateful they showed up in our lives.

# Acknowledgements

My deepest thanks to my house-sitting hosts during this period, and to their various four-legged darlings: Woody, Chloe, Buddy, Indy, Bebe, Stella, Smags, Teo, Sam & Willow. Jo and I are both huge animal lovers, and we've fallen in love with several of 'our' pets along the way. One or two have even inspired songs.

Thanks to cousins Sue Fitz and Nicky Fitz for their love and hospitality; Swati, Linda, and Stacey, soul sisters, always; Brian and Claire of *Pilgrims* in Glastonbury; and William Young, the chauffeur.

My children are uppermost in my heart and mind in everything I do, especially when it's just a little too crazy even for me. I love you both so much. In fact, I idolise you. You're amazing. I'm so glad you've both got the travel and adventure bug – it's the best thing.

I barely know where to start to thank Jo. Jo is probably the gentlest and softest person I know, with a massive core of love and healing ability, and she is inherently a conduit for whatever Light is around to be channelled. It was a joy to spend this time with her and a thrill to be a part of the work she was doing. We traversed three countries and several hundred miles of our souls together. We propped each other up, poured drinks and made cups of tea for each other, cloaked each other in love and kindness, and straight-talked each other a few times too. I drove, Jo navigated, the Marys provided the map. It was, and is, a powerful combination.

Jo also contributed several key parts to this book: the cover art, the story of Hathor and Sekhmet, and several other memories of moments and experiences I'd forgotten. She's provided important editorial support and the story would quite literally not have been written without her.

Best friends usually develop over time, but Jo was an old friend before we'd even met.

# About the Author

Sue Fitzmaurice has been a nurse, business owner, management consultant, CEO, and personal coach. She has a lifetime's interest in international politics and all religions, and has degrees in philosophy & political science, international relations & international law, and business. A native of New Zealand, her adult children still live in Wellington; she now travels the world. She has a novel, *Angels in the Architecture*, and two non-fiction books on the topic of purpose. *The Accidental Mary Pilgrimage* is the first of three unusual travelogues being released in 2018.

www.suefitzmaurice.com

Made in the USA
San Bernardino, CA
06 July 2018